T0374452

Elephant

Joan Cofrancesco

authorHOUSE®

AuthorHouse™
1663 Liberty Drive
Bloomington, IN 47403
www.authorhouse.com
Phone: 1 (800) 839-8640

Published by AuthorHouse 05/31/2017

ISBN: 978-1-5246-9422-7 (sc)
ISBN: 978-1-5246-9421-0 (e)

joan cofrancesco obituary

she once dreamt about hitler's mustache

she thought all the cool people are in hell

she loved the smell of wet cedar
after stacking wood
and the sun breaking
through dark clouds
with the colors of a turner landscape

if her house caught fire she'd run out clutching
photos poetry and her cat bob

she loved the ladies
whose skin was as soft as
a brancusi statue

she felt at home everywhere

her sheets were often in disarray

she has taken zeppelin's stairway to heaven

bloody tower london
guide counting heads
as we exit

ice on my windowpanes
last piece of cherry wood in the stove
and my cat beside me
warm
all night

the 7 year old elmer-glued
a red crayon cat
onto a piece of blue construction paper
so sure that's where it belongs

in the zendo
i took off my shoes
be still
someone said
i put my shoes back on

i walk down bleeker
to the white horse tavern
i want what dylan thomas had

late winter
in my a frame in the adirondacks
drinking black coffee
imagination blooming
like the aspen
like the cedar
like the pine

you are naked
on all 4's
let's do it
pussy style

we all still want
to come out
in a Pocket Book

on hardwood floor
white cat
on black panties

janis croons heartbreak
of southern comfort

2 white figures fucking
on a wall in pompeii
their dog still chained to a post

after skiing
i come home
light a fire
drink hot sake
and watch you
masturbate

remember
the left bank
i bought
char's *leaves of hypnos*
we held hands
and walked
into the absinthe night

duet

rain on the roof
quill on rice paper

hail hitting my skin
and i don't mind
leaving your house
you still naked under warm covers

watching you laying naked
on cool lavender sheets—
no telling
how many more poems
i can write

candle shadows
dancing on the wall
bottle of sake in my belly
no thoughts
about tomorrow

the guy downstairs blasts
sweet home alabama
i'm on the roof in august
guzzling beer

fire popping spruce
i chant baudelaire
and sip brandy all night
watching the smoke and moon
lavender candle burning
coltrane on the stereo
slow kisses
all one special afternoon

poem to paul claudel

he stains my soul
like ink

faded jeans
red flannel shirt
retired
plenty of time

corso's *gasoline*
in my right back pocket
i walk to his grave
in rome
next to shelley's

child's drawing
of the ocean and sea
with him sitting on top

poem to sonia sanchez

i was in casablanca
no bogie no bergman
just a jacuzzi a moon and you
cows meander in a field
cars going fifty
each way

she curls up
under my fur blanket
i hold her in the warmth of our bed
a stray cat screams far off
a full moon

vacation
strolling with you
along the seine
then sitting under
an olive tree
in umbria
reading proust
sipping wine
i don't want
to go back
to ny

i spent 400 dollars
on a black leather jacket
before going to europe
cause i wanted to be a poet?
even emily knew better than that

walpurgis night
our thighs slither
on my black satin sheets

drinking coors on the porch
night in the catskills

smoking a joint
reading *evergreen review*
propped up on
your naked leg wrapped around me

nude photo of you
stuck in my book
the art of happiness

bone tired
my cat beside me
i read haikus
then wake up still
holding the book
cat on my chest
staring at me

lovemaking all day
blanket of snow
surrounding our cabin

closed minds
monday thru friday

llamas and yaks
can hike the himalayas
but not this 2-legged joan

zsa zsa
queen from outer space
strutting
in your glamorous gowns
while your assistants
in bright colored
mini-skirts
low cleavage shirts
high heels
waved oversized
rayguns around

rimbaud ran off to africa
and got syph
lorca got shot by spanish soldiers
berryman jumped off a bridge
morrison od'd in a tub in paris
plath offed herself in an oven
sexton co'd herself in a garage
what was i thinking
when i decided to become a poet

i sip black russians all afternoon
look at mapplethorpes
cocks and balls
leather and chains
now this is what i call art

under the cedars
his axe rings down
on a pine
soon smoke will rise
above the snow

you'll be wearing
a lennon t-shirt
and i'll be carrying
o'hara poems
we'll smile
stoned and happy
on the streets of paris

naked in the ocean
magic
fully alive
blue sky

and then shark

pompeii marathon
who wants to be stuck
in this running position
for all eternity

simple
i love haiku
a chinese painting
the four notes
of a blues song

first lennon gets killed
then aids comes along
9/11
and trump

midway
some like to ride
the double ferris wheel
and some are content
to eat cotton candy

i walk past
the renoirs klimts and matisses
toward an insignificant man
fishing from a tiny boat
among massive mountains

pablo in rome
finds
huge half naked
romanesque woman
running on the beach

on cnn
terrorism
outside a deer leaps
in october light

creeley poem
throw in a talisman
an amulet
and a quick surprise

smells of coffee and leather
first thing in the morning
smile at me

oh yes she said
i used to write
poetry and draw
in high school
then i got real

flowers by The Wall
at my cousin mike's name

blizzard outside
we wined and sucked
and blazed all night

holstein staring at me
out of state fair barn
wish i could swish a tail
at these flies

september drizzle
the cat's head beneath
the wet maple leaves

in the zen temple
the silence of a stray
black cat

small stone cottage
picking mulberries
cutting branches
then wandering off
to see cheshire cats

li po walked
into my dream
last night
carrying a cat
and a begging bowl
why do you think
you always have to be
happy he asked
remember in
every deep ocean
there is
at least one
tear

she told me
to get out
of her poem

living in the tao
sake
after breakfast
contemplation
of your thighs

t-shirts and socks
in front of
the fireplace
we ski each other
finally

pension air
time to prowl
around bookstores
in my orange hoodie

she wore
a short black dress
turquoise earrings
we drank together
and when she left
my cat and pillow
smelled like shalimar

cat sleeping beside me
the poem
gyms bars and bookstores
a tom looking for sex
teakettle wok beads cats
woodstove cabin in the woods
freedom

you were in
a led zeppelin tee
and tight
jeans
watching a special
and i was watching your legs

10 years old
mason jar filled
with kennedy halves
i was rich

87 west 60th st.
everywhere i turn
is a poem
no need to climb
high peaks anymore

i envied plath and sexton
but i didn't have the nerve

woman beside me
staring at a bruegel
as i stare at her

woodstock
3 nuns walk by
give me the peace sign
and warn me
about the brown acid

in florence
high on
espresso
outdoor cafes
michaelangelo
davinci
botticelli

warhol?
what the hell is he doing here!

breezy saturday evening
she stood naked
in front of the roman bathtub
i was so into my caffe and gelati
i almost missed her

i imagine
a road made
of black satin
sheets draped over
your nude body
and i can't keep
the car on the road

in greece
i got to see
a minotaur
right after
the ouzo

cat poses
i draw
soft pink
seven toes
and a monet blue
pair of eyes

retirement
wake up
have a shot
of apricot brandy
vivaldi and led zeppelin
play with furry bob
and go back to bed

snowstorm
as if sundays
weren't lonely enough

i live
like a taoist hermit
my world war one
aviator's hat
flapping at my ears

provincetown
sun   sea
dunes   bars
art   fucking
god   happy

sitting in lotus
practicing
cat decides to jump
into my lap
then i make tea
take a nap
write 5 poems
cat knows
i can't stay silent
anyway

did rilke's belovd
ever appear
did breton ever sleep
with nadja
did yeats ever nail
beatrice
if they had
imagine
all the great art
we'd have missed

wet with september rain
you remind me of
a medieval saint
otherworldly
content in the moment
mindfully eating
a cherry

drunk
christmas eve mass
i watch the strobing candles
on the altar

your skin tastes like
apples
woodsmoke
maple syrup
upstate ny

7 days of snow
beethoven
woodstove cat
and you

pablo
my russian blue cat
every moment i spend with you
becomes a picasso

matisse's dancers
miles' blue horn
li po on the shelf

after skiing
killington
you slept with me
the same jefferson starship song
playing over and over
if only you believe…

naked bodies
intertwined
on black satin
sheets
dissolving

sipping merlot all night
watching
the sky
light
full moon

subway
behind a bag lady
and a young man
with a cello
i get off

college   a blue room
cemetery outside
beer   verlaine
coke   madness
love

i drink in
hot cidery
winter
trance myself
in bly's snowy fields

cold winter day
go easy on the firewood
keep the poems short

coltrane's horn
foggy as the morning
ocean

fear madness america
plastic money shopping
network

pot &
a vivaldi version
of zeppelin

the first snow
flakes
new york in love

smoking opium
i'm a poet of china
dream

hemingway
cats booze books
picasso sculptures
key west
old man typing
in the sea

i think of you
reefer
music
marley and dancing

i write
on the back of matchbooks
a good poem
should smell of woodfire

new years day
i remain unresolved

old poems
make the woodstove
blaze

i no longer
live the cuckoo
clock-driven life
limbs jerking
like second hands
around the power-mad hours

i fell in love
with writing poems
when i realized how much
they enjoyed talking
to me

i light a candle
burn nag champa incense
sprinkle 3 drops of
blue lotus tincture
in my 4-footed bath tub
sink in
and ride bareback

thunderstorm
pitbull
snuggling
even closer

city lights bookstore
fly on kerouac's
book of haikus

i feel like
a red toy tractor
left on the lawn
in snow

provincetown at night
creeping
cats and lesbians

my cat pablo
a blue cube
with two eyes

plowing
business card
buried in snow

confederate dollar
found in
a used how to get rich book
store

feeding
a stray cat
on halloween
what a treat

garden buddha
wearing
an enormous dress
of autumn leaves

the rabbit's ears
gather more channels

my mason jar
full of pennies
i'm a quarter of the way
to paris

sick
of all
this lake effect
filling tiny clouds
with massive flaky egos

these 33 rpm blues
call for more
kingfisher beer
and panama red

no attachments
to this world
snow melts
in my hand

i'm the queen
of small stuff
stacks of kindling
wool socks
city lights pocket poetry

basho
sipping sake
jumps
into the pond
drowns
and frog emerges

sitting naked
in front of the fire
eating an apple
reading baudelaire
wishing for
nothing

lucky
i strut around
like the reincarnation
of buddha himself
and nobody knows it

reading lowell's *notebook*
sipping bordeaux
listening to vivaldi
smiling
having a great day
then it hits me
fuck...trump is president

coffee
banana
toast
with marmalade
good morning, one of billions!

good luck i whispered
squeezing
my amulet
on a 747 to paris

is that
fresh cut grass
i smell
between your legs?

i worked
the night shift
at the marcellus casket co.
1968
the boys coming back
from nam

when i am left
by a lover
the parting shot
is always
"and nobody cares
about your stupid poetry
anyways!"

lesbians separating:
who will get custody
of the cats!

i walk through
your beaded door
smell of patchouli and pot
haiku spread on the table
with a half full glass of wine
i know i am home

sipping crow
watching you walk
around the kitchen
in your brand new
black lacies
blasting bird bootleg blues
oh please
can i lick the frosting

go poem
stir demons
and spirits
punch them
in the face
pull out rimbaud's pistol
cock it and,
shit, shoot

fat figaro
jumps on me
at 3 in the morning
and starts purring
but i'm not francis of assisi

bottle of brooklyn lager
joint and
concerto for two violins
memories of bach
in the air

cats and books
fall down together
from the shelf—
it takes me awhile
to decide

which japanese poet
was i 300 years ago?
maybe i was the frog

taoist books
all over my bed—
i can't draw worth a fuck

spring cleaning
buddhas and haiku books
sitting on the grass

i'm a mountain woman
red flannel shirt
hiking boots
woodstove blazing
iron butterfly on
shot of jack in my hand

pick any room
where there is a van gogh
and all the other paintings
disappear

sitting on the porch
chimes
of the multi-colored
maple leaves
trees
losing their leaves
still lucky
to be alive

between
cage the elephant
and florence & the machine
i like to listen to
bird and billie

rain
nam
nixon
neil young on
pot smoking in my VW
getting ready to
make a run
to my first class

a night to continue
without end
lying beside you
naked on a bear rug
in front of the fire
giving and getting
backrubs

new turquoise ring
tender chicken
feel good
flannel shirt

sage and sandalwood air
long brown hair and scarves
neither of us knew
it would be
the last time

black crayon
in the gold
and crimson
leaves

wake up
hear *let it be*
read li po
and see basquait

poetry
plum wine
incense
aveda candle
hermit's life

on the fifth floor of
Bird Library
i see *naomi poems corpse and beans*
author page says
"saint geraud
unemployed
not looking for a job"
i take him home

hoarders on tv
crap
accumulation
firewood
poetry
catnip mouse
friend's watercolor
all i need

in the gift shop
i buy a postcard
write a dirty poem
on the back
of the photo
of the vatican

brautigan
and bukowski
gone
nothing good
to read anymore

Printed in the United States
By Bookmasters